T0065495

Other books by this author:

*My Reality Check Bounced: Confessions of a 21st Century Sinner*

*The Little Egg: When Walking on Egg Shells Ain't All It's Cracked Up to Be*

*Coupling: Investing in Relationship*

www.onehipangel.com

www.randikonikoff.com

# LoveSTRONG

*a devotional*

Randi Konikoff, Ph.D.

Copyright © 2021 Randi Konikoff, Ph.D.

All rights reserved. No part of this book may be used or reproduced by any means, graphic, electronic, or mechanical, including photocopying, recording, taping or by any information storage retrieval system without the written permission of the author except in the case of brief quotations embodied in critical articles and reviews.

This book is a work of non-fiction. Unless otherwise noted, the author and the publisher make no explicit guarantees as to the accuracy of the information contained in this book and in some cases, names of people and places have been altered to protect their privacy.

WestBow Press books may be ordered through booksellers or by contacting:

WestBow Press
A Division of Thomas Nelson & Zondervan
1663 Liberty Drive
Bloomington, IN 47403
www.westbowpress.com
844-714-3454

Because of the dynamic nature of the Internet, any web addresses or links contained in this book may have changed since publication and may no longer be valid. The views expressed in this work are solely those of the author and do not necessarily reflect the views of the publisher, and the publisher hereby disclaims any responsibility for them.

Any people depicted in stock imagery provided by Getty Images are models, and such images are being used for illustrative purposes only. Certain stock imagery © Getty Images.

Scripture quotations taken from The Holy Bible, New International Version® NIV® Copyright © 1973 1978 1984 2011 by Biblica, Inc. TM. Used by permission. All rights reserved worldwide.

Scripture taken from The Message. Copyright © 1993, 1994, 1995, 1996, 2000, 2001, 2002. Used by permission of NavPress Publishing Group.

Scripture quotations taken from the (NASB®) New American Standard Bible®, Copyright © 1960, 1971, 1977, 1995, 2020 by The Lockman Foundation. Used by permission. All rights reserved. www.lockman.org

Scripture taken from the Amplified Bible, Copyright © 1954, 1958, 1962, 1964, 1965, 1987 by The Lockman Foundation. Used with permission.

Scripture taken from the Complete Jewish Bible (CJB)® Copyright © 1998 by David H. Stern. Used by permission. All rights reserved.

ISBN: 978-1-6642-2597-8 (sc)
ISBN: 978-1-6642-2598-5 (e)

Library of Congress Control Number: 2021904483

Print information available on the last page.

WestBow Press rev. date: 03/12/2021

# Dedications

Thank you to the special people in my life who helped with editing and encouragement.

To my children, Peaches, Emerald and Elijah, who have taught me that love never runs out, who have continued to love me even at my most unlovable and who make it so easy for me to love them.

My puppy, Teddy, who shows me nothing but love.

Dedicated to my LORD and Savior, Jesus Christ, who demonstrated his love for us in that while we were yet sinners he died for us. It took me 36 years to finally get it. Thank you for never giving up on me.

Thank you.

# From the Author

I do not consider myself a writer, but more of a word photographer or a chef, whipping together a one and done experience for the senses. My mind goes too fast to hold a single thought for more than a page at a time.

So here you have tidbits, the shortest of stories, to capture your attention and inspire you to take it from there. Enjoy each morsel as a sample from my mental charcuterie board. Bon appetite.

Otherwise known as "Randi-isms', take a peek inside the mind and the life of a survivor of single parenting, domestic violence, the music business, corporate America, anti-semitism, trauma, addiction and a life that's been totally transformed by God's love.

# Foreword

My wife and I have been blessed to share Randi Konikoff's journey for over two decades. We have known her on good days and bad - through celebration and heartbreak – laughter and tears. The result of enduring all that life has to throw at you is that you become real, genuine and authentic. Others can see what you are made of. In referencing one of Randi's and my favorite stories, just like Margery Williams writes in her classic, *The Velveteen Rabbit*, with each passing day, the Rabbit becomes a little more worn – but that's what it is to be real, genuine, honest and authentic. Being "real" means that others can see what you are made of.

I can tell you that when God made Randi, He gave her a tender heart for others. He made her to be kind and compassionate. She knows what it is to break and so she cares all the more for the broken. Along the way, God has deepened her sense of empathy and given her a great capacity for wisdom and spiritual guidance. She is a gifted speaker, writer, counselor and friend...because she is real.

I am confident that this devotional guide will be a blessing to you and to your family. Please ponder it, pray on it and process these thoughts. And know that these "Randi-isms" emanate from the spiritual journey of a true Velveteen Rabbit.

Frank A. Mercer
Senior Pastor, Rolling Hills Baptist Church
Executive Director, FireChaplain.org

2 Corinthians 4: [7] But we have this treasure in jars of clay to show that this all-surpassing power is from God and not from us. [8] We are hard pressed on every side, but not crushed; perplexed, but not in despair; [9] persecuted, but not abandoned; struck down, but not destroyed. [16] Therefore we do not lose heart. Though outwardly we are wasting away, yet inwardly we are being renewed day by day. [17] For our light and momentary troubles are achieving for us an eternal glory that far outweighs them all. [18] So we fix our eyes not on what is seen, but on what is unseen, since what is seen is temporary, but what is unseen is eternal.

# Preface

How this book came to be...

I was having my quiet time, meditating on the Word, when God directed my thoughts to how unloving I have been toward myself. Like most women, I had an unending supply of criticisms and put downs in my arsenal against my physical body. This particular morning God had me thinking about the power of his love. He encouraged me to experiment with committing to completely loving myself for one whole day. Dedicate one day to speaking and thinking only positive words and thoughts toward and about myself. The results were life changing for me. It did not stop with just the physical body, but spilled over into every area of my life. This book came out of that experiment. My prayer is that you will allow God to fill you with the life changing power of his love.

*Randi*

Here is the original experiment:

*For the rest of today, love everything about your body. Instead of putting yourself down and criticizing yourself, look at your body with love. Love your feet and toes, for without them you could not sing "This Little Piggy." Love your legs that work so hard for you all day. Love your arms that get to hug your loved ones. Love your skin that lets you enjoy feeling everything from snowflakes to sand castles. Love your ears that allow you to hear the voices that mean so much to you and listen to the music that lifts your spirit. Love your eyes that bring the world around you into your mind. Love your exquisite mind for the amazing ability to reason, to imagine and to create the life you are blessed to be given. Love every last wrinkle on your face, adding to the tapestry of your life. Even love your jiggly upper arms, your squishy thighs, your love handles and your double chin. Love everything about your body. Think kindly about yourself, treat yourself well and just see how your mood changes. You are so much more than just a body. Experience the change that takes place within you when you elevate yourself in love. Imagine how differently you may feel about others when you come from a place of acceptance with yourself.*

# Table of Contents

*love*

# Accentuates

*Love magnifies everything it touches.*
*When I act lovingly toward myself,*
*I find I have more love for others.*
*Being loving toward myself extends love and expands love outwardly. When I give, I gain.*

## Stay Calm and Give On

Anxiety compromises and lowers your immune system. You don't have to be as old as I am to be concerned about this. One way to lower anxiety is to get out of your own way. Think of others, do for others.

Givers gain in many ways. The giving and gaining can be felt in many ways. Do you know people who need their medicine picked up from the pharmacy and brought to them? Can you spare a square? Can you bring supplies to your neighbor's doorstep? Can you order meals to be delivered to friends? Can you video call loved ones and spread positivity? Can you write emails, letters or cards thanking people for ways they have encouraged or inspired you?

What do you gain? Immeasurable rewards in neurochemistry. Research has proven that when we give to others we reap emotional health benefits that are greater and last longer than when we merely give to ourselves.

With the undisputed research supporting thoughts as energy, direct your thoughts, prayers and efforts toward lifting us all up and through this unprecedented time.

Give, and it will be given to you. A good measure, pressed down, shaken together and running over, will be poured into your lap. For with the measure you use, it will be measured to you. (Luke 6:38)

**Date:** ______________________________

**Reflections:**

*love*

# Never Breaks

***We try it out, we try it on, we approach with caution. We inch up as close as we can to get a better look. As vast as the Grand Canyon, as powerful as Niagara Falls. Fear may feel deep and wide, but love's rewards are immeasurable.***

## What Remains

I just had the sweetest red bell pepper. Hang in here with me even if you don't like red bell peppers. There's a lesson to be learned. This pepper was juicy, the color was vibrant, the crunch was satisfying and the flavor was delicious. I would go so far as to say I can actually feel my cells smiling. A few weeks ago, I made some major changes to the food I'd been consuming. Here's the lesson: when we take something away, after the initial struggle to recalibrate, we heighten the impact of what remains.

Now, let's unpack. Have you ever had a stomach virus? After the sick stomach and the vomiting stop, there's this oasis of peace. A reprieve from the nausea. Ask any woman in labor about those moments between contractions. Or the thwarted sneeze that finally explodes. Decreasing added sugar from your food. Eliminating worry and anxiety from your thoughts. What remains in each case? The natural working of our digestive system, the restoration of physical comfort, satisfaction after the release of the sneeze, enhanced taste from foods and a sense of peace.

Remember the lesson? When we take something away, after the initial struggle to recalibrate, we heighten the impact of what remains. In the case of removing anxiety from our lives, we gain an awareness of what is within our control and what is not. Stop 'kicking against the goads' (Acts 26:14b) and come to an acceptance of reality as the first step to change. We must face reality in order to focus on what *is* and effectively work out the issue from there. Fighting against reality is refusing to accept facts and living in a false realm. It's like dropping a penny and expecting it to fall *up*.

This third I will put into the fire; I will refine them like silver and test them like gold. They will call on my name and I will answer them; I will say, 'They are my people,' and they will say, 'The Lord is our God.'" (Zechariah 13:9)

**Date:** ____________________

**Reflections:**

# *love* Collaborates

*Love creates something that cannot exist apart from what it joins together. A melody and a harmony that captivate the world. A song of love. And the world instinctively knows every note.*

## Sandwiched in Sessions

My clients are in various stages of change and different levels of insightfulness. What a blessing it is to be present in a session when a client is able to see the humor in their own dysfunctional thinking and laugh heartily as they emerge from the jail cell that's been holding them captive! Freedom is sweet and the release of self-imposed restrictions and rules is life-giving!

While some are much more profound, a recent session had my client "ROFL" at his own rigid rules involving sandwiches. Years of confrontation and marital discord were laid to rest as he recognized and willfully let go of his immovable stance that mayonnaise goes on the cheese side and mustard goes on the meat side! When I asked if the sandwich tasted differently when made contrary to his rule, he looked at me as though I had green hair. The next moment he burst out laughing, which then led to tears of joy.

Another client expressed deep frustration over her husband's stubborn refusal to concede to her way of placing the silverware in the dishwasher. Years of arguments and sleeping with backs to each other over the direction of flatware!

It actually has little to do with sandwiches and silverware. It has everything to do with pride. When our need to be right surpasses our commitment to our marriage, we are drawing battle lines, amassing troops, and preparing for war. Your spouse is not your adversary. Think of how different life could be if we could see the humor in our preferences and have fun with them. Mondays, Wednesdays and Fridays, put the silverware in facing down! Tuesdays, Thursdays and Saturdays, face up! Sundays, hand wash the dishes together and enjoy the time with each other.

Years of prideful interaction can develop thick scar tissue on the heart, which is difficult to penetrate. Far too many individuals choose to place their pride above their marriage. Far too many marriages fall prey to separation and divorce and far too many children are put through this painful transition.

Commitment to God, marriage, children - in that order - will keep us humble, focused, and positioned to be blessed with loving families who can laugh, cry, and serve others together.

And let us consider how we may spur one another on toward love and good deeds, (Hebrews 10:24)

**Date:** ______________________

**Reflections:**

# *love*

# Demonstrates

***Witnessing an expression of love is the ultimate teaching moment. The observer, the giver and the recipient are all profoundly affected by the experience.***

## He's My Daddy

I was just a little girl, growing up the youngest of four in 1960's New York. Having no choice in the selection of my family, I won the Family Lottery. Daddy was charismatic and renown and Momma was beautiful and bold.

I've always felt that one of the greatest gifts I received from my daddy was his last name. It was what he created out of that name that made a difference in my life. Back in the 60's and 70's, it was a common occurrence for me to go anywhere and be asked, "Are you related to Eli?" With great pride I would smile and whisper, "Yes, he's my daddy."

As a kid, this held tremendous influence on me. Now I imagine you are thinking about the influence this had on how people treated me, but I meant on my own behavior. Early on, I realized that anything I said or did would reflect on that name. Once people knew who my daddy was, who I represented, I would be judged as a reflection of that name, of my daddy.

Eli was my earthly daddy. I wish you could have known him. Larger than life, a man of the people. His strong hands were calloused but warm, strong and loving. God is my heavenly daddy. I pray you would know him. He rules over life, the Creator of all people. His strong hands are scarred but his arms are open wide, warm strong and loving.

I know that one of the greatest gifts I have ever received from my heavenly daddy is his name. I am a Messianic Christian. It is what Christ did for me that has made all the difference in my life. Now, when people learn that I am a Christian I am aware that anything I say or do will reflect on that name. I will be judged as a reflection of that name, of my heavenly daddy.

When circumstances, trials and tribulation come along in my life, I have the promise and the protection of my heavenly daddy. I can call upon my faith in my daddy's provision to stand before me and beside me. I can remind my trouble and myself that it will be well with my soul because, "He's my daddy."

Dear children, let us not love with words or speech but with actions and in truth. (1 John 3:18)

**Date:** ______________________

**Reflections:**

# *love*

# Exhilarates

***Love is like grasping a handful of helium balloons, lifting you off the ground in one sweeping movement. Your feet never touch the ground in the same way again. Your heart finds a new rhythm and the thrill of living is restored and renewed.***

## Brainstorming versus Worrying

Imagine a large corporation calling an emergency meeting with all of the highest-level executives and stockholders. Flying them in from various cities and countries around the world. Travel arrangements, hotel reservations being made, limos and car services at the ready to provide transportation from the airport to the meeting location. An elaborate spread of pastries, juices, coffees, ice water. Whiteboards, Smart Boards, legal pads, pens, pencils. Phone and computer chargers beside each genuine leather ergonomic chair, strategically placed around a magnificent conference room table.

Everyone arrives, takes their place at the table and the meeting facilitator rises to call the meeting to order. "Ladies and gentlemen, thank you so much for coming on such short notice. We have an important and pressing issue we are facing as a company. You have all been made aware of the details. We have arranged to spend 3 hours together today to focus on this issue and only on this issue. So, commence worrying."

Can you imagine calling a meeting to worry? What a waste of resources, time, money and energy. What a ridiculous concept. Yet, each time we find ourselves worrying over something we are imitating that exact same scene. We have called a meeting to worry. Worrying accomplishes nothing productive. Worrying is an anxiety producing behavior choice which does nothing to solve the problem but does much to convolute the worrier, rendering him or her helpless.

Instead of worrying, if you must spend time ruminating over a topic or issue, replace worry with brainstorming. Brainstorming is more productive, takes up less time and produces a list of alternative solutions. Brainstorming leaves you with a feeling of accomplishment even if the problem still exists.

Worrying is constricting and chokes out any creativity, prolonging the problem and heightening the anxiety level. Brainstorming expands the mind and affords an opportunity for unrestricted creative thinking. One action is depleting and damaging. The other is energizing and life-giving.

Make a conscious choice to change your worrying into brainstorming. Your problem and your mood will thank you for it.

May the God of hope fill you with all joy and peace as you trust in him, so that you may overflow with hope by the power of the Holy Spirit. (Romans 15:13)

**Date:** ______________________________

**Reflections:**

*love*

# Facinates

***Love cannot be explained nor can it be denied. It is exquisitely enticing, drawing us into its spell. Taking us to the highest heights, sustaining us in its updraft. Soaring on its wings, delighting in a view of life that comes into focus with intoxicating clarity.***

## Upward Dog

My puppy loves to lay outside on the back patio. I purposely have a postage stamp size backyard and it's just perfect for my puppy and me. Our little slice of heaven. A little slice of heaven is still heaven. Teddy settles himself down, rejecting the shade created by the umbrella, opting to bathe in the warmth of the sun. He takes in the songs of the birds, the buzzing of the bees and the intermittent offensive roar of the air conditioner. Every so often a refreshing breeze can be felt as it blows across the patio. The movement of the leaves and of the umbrella, along with the pleasant sensation, prove its existence. A sweet release, a cooling off, a time of refreshing. I love that moment when the breeze controls the experience. Whatever I'm thinking and whatever I'm working on shifts in priority as my senses respond to this lovely awakening.

One day, I happened to look over at Teddy just as this breeze invited us to partake of its gift. From his prone position, he lifted his head, arched his neck all the way back and closed his eyes. Giving himself completely over to the experience, he held that pose until the breeze had passed. Oh, to be in the moment like that! You might say that it's easy for a dog to feel complete peace. They don't have the pressures and responsibilities we do. They don't have to forage for food or worry about shelter. True, and no one sends me the human equivalent of his BarkBox delivery every month. However, even with our struggles, that breeze is there for us as much as it is for Teddy. We get to choose if we're going to enjoy it or ignore it.

How many other significant Gifts of the Moment are we choosing to ignore? When was the last time you attended the absolutely free Spectacular in the Sky, two shows daily, 365 days a year? The next time you find yourself about to eat your favorite food, pause to savor the flavor, the texture, the aroma and the experience. How long has it been since you took the hand of your loved one and quietly held it, feeling all the love and life force combining with yours? If you are blessed to have a loved one with whom you can hold hands, remember that there are those who do not and who ache for human touch.

Our Creator has enhanced our ability to feel joy, given us the tools to augment our mundane day to day and the capacity to squeeze every last drop out of each experience. Why? Simply because he loves us and life can be beautiful. Yes, even in the midst of chaos life can be beautiful. Because he lives life can be beautiful. Because he loves me life can be beautiful.

Let the beauty of our LORD be upon us. (Psalm 90:17)

**Date:** ______________________________

**Reflections:**

*love*

# Germinates

***Love in action does not lessen as it is dispensed. It defies the law of diminishing returns. The more it is expressed the more it grows. Its roots burrow down deep and its branches multiply.***

## The Law of Increasing Returns

After writing a song I usually have an overwhelming fear that I may never be able to write another. And yet, 'in the passage of time', I am blessed with the next one. I equate songwriting to conception and birth. There is an emotion, a moment, a spark, a seed, a spontaneous energy that previously did not exist and, after a period of germination, a musical composition is born.

This thought struck me the other day. There are only 12 notes - in various octaves, but only 12 notes. In all the years of musical creation, in all the genres, we have yet to run out of songs. Thousands of years of song writing, countless composers, incalculable numbers of songs and still more and more are written every day. Just think of the Billboard 100 and the Top 40 from every month of every year that you have existed. Think of the most popular songs from ages past that we never even hear anymore.

It got me thinking of things we never run out of. Music, art, literature, medical advancements, inventions, Star Wars sequels and love. We never run out of love. I can't keep enough chocolate in my candy drawer, but I never run out of love. We love our first child and can't imagine loving anything more. We have another and BAM! Our capacity for love has not diminished but doubled! We love our pets and they die. We risk loving one again and BAM! Our love takes on a whole new shape, but equally as strong.

Other things that fall under the category of love are gratefulness, kindness, forgiveness, generosity and grace. These emotions and subsequent acts are rivers of love and deep wells that never run dry.

We live in a society of 'more'. More money, more youth, more food, more toys, more sex, more power. All of those pursuits are bottomless pits, creating an increased desire that will never be satiated.

Love is an enigma. It is the only resource that creates more of itself the more it's used. It is the ultimate return on investment. Brain studies have shown that the pleasure derived from doing something for someone else is greater and lasts longer than doing something just for yourself. We are neurologically hard-wired for love.

Princess Leia was wrong. Obi-Wan is not our only hope. Love is.

Like newborn babies, crave pure spiritual milk, so that by it you may grow up in your salvation. (1 Peter 2:2)

**Date:** ______________________________

**Reflections:**

*love*

# Habituates

***Love is to sink into, fold into, become accustomed to. Is there anything more comforting than familiarity? Your touch, your scent, your gaze, the way our hands intertwine. When I am with my love, I am home.***

## Pause for Paws

I am dog sitting this week. Eva is a very sweet rescue dog, with severe attachment disorder. Perhaps that's why my friends asked me to sit for them. Eva is not content with just sitting near you or beside you. Eva must be sitting on you.

If it was possible, I believe she would hold you down with her paws. Instead, she holds you down with her most powerful weapon – her eyes. Oh, those eyes: two big, black pools of bottomless longing. There is such fear in there. During a recent thunderstorm she actually crawled in the dryer and hid among the warm sheets and towels. Eva needs. She needs security, safety, attention, affection, comfort and kindness. She, like all of us, was made with the capacity to give love and the desire to be cared for.

Our fears may not drive us to crawl into the dryer, but they do drive us, nonetheless. We aren't as transparent as dogs, who can't help but show their emotions through that wagging tail: that barometer of happiness. You know just where you stand with a dog. We, however, have developed the art of pretense. We value it so much that we actually refer to it as an art. You can be talking to me face to face and I may be as smooth as glass on the outside, but on the inside I am a raging storm.

Once Eva settles down on my lap, I let her stay there and notice that in a few minutes her breathing slows down and she rests her head on my knees. Calmness washes over her. If you have someone in your life who makes you feel that way, cherish them and let them know. If you are that someone, that's a gift and you need to use it generously.

You will increase my honor and comfort me once more.
(Psalm 71:21)

**Date:**

**Reflections:**

*love*

# Initiates

***Love takes over and makes its presence known. It demands attention and commands intention. It is a leader, not a follower. And when it is there, everything changes.***

## Purpose in the Pain

Saying goodbye. Leaving something you love. Ending a chapter in your life. Having to push yourself forward into the unknown. The past grips your heart, the present is painful, the future is a mystery, but the Father is faithful.

These are the moments of walking on tiptoes of trust through mine fields of fear. God doesn't stand on the other side of the journey. He doesn't stand off to the side or a few steps ahead. He has crafted each place your foot touches and gently guides you from within.

The greatest example of purpose in the pain is Christ's sacrificial death for each of us on Calvary's cross. The greatest pain and the greatest purpose ever fulfilled. When we have pain, God has not left us. Trust your Savior. He tells us that in this life we will have pain and experience sorrow, but he has given us irreplaceable, indispensable, irrefutable joy. Joy, that goes by the name of Jesus Christ. Joy that is accessible to all who are willing to experience the pain of acknowledging our own limitations for the purpose of accepting God's awesome authority, provision and peace.

People talk about how there is so much pain in the world. Most of us try to avoid pain at all costs. But pain can be a great motivator. Sorry to disagree, Karl Marx, but ease and complacency are the real opium of the people. Simply stated, neuroscience explains how our mind sends signals to our brain, which then sends neuro chemical signals to our body. When we sense something is off, not right, or not working for us, we feel uncomfortable. This discomfort can come in the form of physical pain or emotional pain. A toothache prompts us to see a dentist. A hunger pain motivates us to eat. An empty feeling in our soul leads us to search for meaning. Ecclesiastes 3:11 says that God has set eternity in the hearts of man.

As our Creator, God has instilled in us the knowledge of Him. So, when you feel empty, disconnected, or pained for any reason, let this motivate you to "call as my heart grows faint; lead me to the rock that is higher than I." Psalm 61:2. So, in a world where the ground under my feet is anything but solid, and where foundational truths are being rewritten daily to justify behavior, it is comforting to remember I can cling to the Rock of Ages.

Trust in ADONAI forever, because in Yah ADONAI, is a Rock of Ages. (Isaiah 26:4 CJB)

**Date:** ______________________________

**Reflections:**

*love*

# Jubilates

*Love is triumphant. It always wins.*
*It is the weapon to end all conflicts.*
*It is the hero, the voice of reason,*
*the annihilator of anxiety*
*and the destroyer of*
*despair. Victorious.*

## Eternal Joy

Firefighters experience daily what the rest of the world now feels after watching the Cathedral of Notre Dame, a masterpiece of French Gothic architecture, nearly desecrated before our eyes. Once majestic, sacredly symbolic, irreplaceable, now in peril. If you had the pleasure of seeing it for yourself, you never have forgotten that feeling of awe as its magnificence took your breath away. If you have only seen pictures and heard of its renown, you are impressed by the strength and solidarity it projected.

It took over 800 years to build and was compromised in a matter of hours. We are mourning the loss of its beauty and its symbolic significance, as well we should. Individuals poured their lives into this structure and into the treasures contained within its walls.

We weep for the loss of the tangible, but we can rejoice in the existence of the eternal! The One for whom this spiritual structure was built, the One for whom each artisan was inspired to create, the One for whom each worshipper entered its glorious sanctuary and the One for whom we owe our lives and our eternities, is alive and lives in us! Let this be a challenge to each of us. Spread the Word. Remind the world that we have a living Savior who has conquered death and destruction. Because he lives we can face tomorrow.

The God who made the world and everything in it is the Lord of heaven and earth and does not live in temples built by human hands. And he is not served by human hands, as if he needed anything. Rather, he himself gives everyone life and breath and everything else. (Acts 17:24)

**Date:** ______________________________

**Reflections:**

*love*

# Korrects Mistakes

*Love is True North.*
*It is the only compass you will ever need. It will always, always, lead you home. Love will erase errors and open the doors for forgiveness and grace.*

## For the Giving

There are things for which we have never forgiven ourselves. Living under the weight of regret, guilt or shame. Constantly running our fingers back and forth over the scar.

We convince ourselves that this self-flagellation will ensure no repeat performance. However, living like this keeps us in a continual state of hypervigilance. Don't mess up, don't do that again, stop thinking about that, watch what you say. Checking our thoughts and behaviors, tripping over our next move and always second-guessing ourselves.

Meanwhile we're too busy in defense mode to enjoy life, to be authentic. How can we be ourselves when we don't trust ourselves to be ourselves?

There is true forgiveness, beyond our capacity to invoke or fully understand. But it's available to all. Come out from underneath all that weight and experience the freedom you are meant to have. As the hymn says, Jesus paid it all. All to him I owe. Sin had left a crimson stain. He washed it white as snow.*

*Jesus Paid it All, Elvina M. Hall

When he had received the drink, Jesus said, "It is finished." With that, he bowed his head and gave up his spirit. (John 19:30)

Date: ______________________________

Reflections:

# *love*

# Liberates

***Love frees the captives. Whether incarcerated behind lock and key or a prison of your own making, Love has the power to set you free.***

## Your Shirt's Not Green

Some of us are heavily influenced by statements and judgements others make to or about us. What contributes to our insecurities may be an underlying fear that what they are saying is true - that they actually are right and we are wrong. This false belief can be so permeating that we may actually live out our days in such fear of being wrong that we anticipate these judgements and trip over ourselves in our attempts to prevent it.

What plunges us deeper into self-doubt and self-deprivation is when we lack a strong enough belief in ourselves and our own truth.

Do you understand that you do not have to take everything someone else tells you as fact? Pretty much everything, and I mean everything, that someone says to you (and you back to them) is filtered through that individual's perspective.

Let's say that you happen to be wearing a blue shirt as you're reading this. If someone came up to you and said,

"Listen, I have to tell you that I really have a problem with that green shirt you are wearing.

It is actually the ugliest green I have ever seen and I do not like it at all!" What would your response be to that? Would you be horrified, embarrassed and run to your closet to change your clothes?

First, you may think, "Wow, somebody is obviously color blind." But I doubt your feelings would be hurt or that you would ruminate for the next three days over it. Here's why...Your shirt's not green. You know that your shirt's not green. You don't believe your shirt is green. You know and believe that your shirt is not green, it's blue. You know it's blue, you believe it's blue. You are completely secure in your belief.

We aren't rattled or bothered or shaken by statements we do not believe are true. However, when we place the value of other's opinions over our own and allow them to cause us to question our own truth, that is when we are vulnerable to drown under the tsunami of self-ridicule. Know who you are and whose you are and you will not be subject to questioning your value and worth.

Being secure in who you are in Christ is the foundation for Biblical caring for others. God does not want us to put the needs of others a head of our own as an unhealthy way to EARN love and acceptance. We are truly free to see the value and worth in others once we are secure in the knowledge of it in ourselves.

...until we all reach unity in the faith and in the knowledge of the Son of God, as we mature to the full measure of the stature of Christ. Then we will no longer be infants, tossed about by the waves and carried around by every wind of teaching and by the clever cunning of men in their deceitful scheming. (Ephesians 4:13-14)

**Date:** ______________________

**Reflections:**

*love*

# Mediates

*Love softens the hardest of hearts. Melting conflict and allowing each side to grant asylum. Providing safety and security and paving the road to restoration.*

## Myopia

I'm having to get used to wearing glasses - the kind that make you want to rip them off and hurl them against the wall. They used to call them bifocals. I call them 'You gotta hold your head just right or you wanna throw up' glasses. "Oh, you'll get the hang of it", offered the smiling ophthalmologist. Oh yeah? I look like a human bobble head, desperately trying to find that sweet spot hidden somewhere between blurry and blurrier. I am told that the brain is responsible for interpreting what the eyes see. Right now my brain is screaming, "Take these things off – I was doing better without them!" My head is moving around so much, I'm liable to pull a neck muscle.

Sometimes I wrestle more with the solution than I do with the problem! If you're like me, someone who has a hard time accepting help, we rebel against the most considerate and loving gestures. I used to drive a Jeep Wrangler and would leave the windows off all the time in the summer. They were a tremendous pain to zip on and off, so I would just put up with the weather. One night I was at work and my Jeep was parked in the uncovered parking lot. A raging thunder storm came through and I dreaded the soaking wet seat I would have to face. When I walked out that night, I was shocked to see that all the windows had been put on my Jeep!

It could only have been one particular angel who would have come out in the middle of that storm to do such an act of kindness. Instead of being grateful, though, I was furious. Instead of accepting this as an act of sacrificial love, my traumatized past interpreted it as a slam against my ability to take care of myself. I mistook compassion for criticism. Talk about looking a gift horse in the mouth!

So, my interpretation of things used to be like these glasses. I was interpreting things from my blurry, defensive mind. With these glasses, if I tilt my head or shift my focus, I can see clearly. Shifting my focus off of myself and on to Jesus has helped me clear my vision in so many areas of my life. The more time I spend with him, and get used to him as my focus, the more comfortable and natural it becomes to rely on him for complete clarity and guidance.

While my physical sight may be deteriorating, my spiritual insight is increasing daily. Looking to and through the mercy and grace of my Savior is my prescription for healthier vision and a healthier life.

...knowing him personally, your eyes focused and clear...
(Ephesians 1:18 The Message)

**Date:** ______________________

**Reflections:**

*love*

# Navigates

***The stormiest seas, the foggiest nights, the most misunderstood discussions can all be rescued. Love is the light to help you find your way and guide you back to where you belong.***

## The Spring of Our Discontent

On January 1, 2020 we awoke to the promises of a new year. 2020 - a year, by its very definition, suggesting clarity, greater vision and new perspective. Launching full speed ahead into healthier eating, exercise commitments, social interactions, traveling and unparalleled accomplishments, many of us lamented 2019 but chose to focus on the prospects of a brighter 2020. A new year, a new beginning, a fresh start.

Just as the ice and snow were fading into memory and the darkness of Daylight Savings Time gave way to Spring, we took a sucker punch below the belt that sent us down for the count. A haymaker that landed and was felt 'round the world. Everything stopped. Stop, in the name of glove. And mask. Then the surreal became the so real. While we hid at home it began to hit home. This wasn't something happening on the other side of the world. This was happening to the entire world. We sheltered in place as Passover arrived, reminding us of the lamb's blood and the Angel of Death. A new term, 'social distancing' kept us from corporately celebrating resurrection and new life. Businesses tweaked, TeleHealth peaked and Wall Street shrieked.

But the best of humanity refuses to be held down. It rises like a phoenix from the ashes. Individuals push through the impact on their personal lives and come to the aid and rescue of others. When all the material things, schedules and trappings of the world are torn away, what not only remains but flourishes is the human spirit. Reminding us that in the worst of times, we are resilient and resourceful. We get hit hard, there is damage, there is loss, but there is hope. There is humanity. We can persevere and we can choose to come out of this richer for the experience.

This pandemic is a powerful equalizer. We will all be changed. We have the potential to be infected with compassion. We can heal from self-centered lifestyles and we can recover from myopic vision. When it comes to life, we are all in this together. You are not in my way, we are here for each other. Maybe we had to be separated in order to realize just how much we need each other.

More than oil, more than money, our greatest commodity is love. It is limitless, costs nothing to produce and grows stronger the more you give it away. It is our greatest natural resource. When all is said and done, it's not how we lived, but how we loved.

And now these three remain: faith, hope and love. But the greatest of these is love. (1 Corinthians 13:13)

**Date:**

**Reflections:**

# *love*

# Operates

***Love is not afraid to attack dis-ease, removing any obstacle in its way. Balancing surgical precision with compassion. Tenderly cleansing the wound. Though a scar may remain, the healing begins.***

# The Spot

Parking is permitted on one side of the street in my neighborhood. There are signs posted to indicate where parking begins and where it ends. That first spot, the one closest to the sign, has been silently touted as the Prince of Parking Spaces. It shall heretofore be known as 'the spot.' How do I know this? By witnessing the spectacular lengths at which my neighbors vie for and jockey for this coveted position.

I park in my garage, so I am not a participant in this blood sport, but I am a spectator. My home office faces the street and I have divinely been awarded preferred seating. While the comings and goings of my neighbors holds no interest for me, the battle for 'the spot' is a highly enjoyable study in human behavior.

I begin my day by opening the blinds and observing the winner from the previous night. He or she who secures the spot for the entire night has bragging rights and, no doubt, sleeps with a satisfactory smile on their face. But the victory is short-lived, as the pressure begins again with the start of each new parking day.

Those who work from home have a court advantage over those who must vacate 'the spot' as necessary to make their living. One neighbor actually moves his car from spots of shame further down the street into ‘the spot’, exiting the vehicle with a look of pride and a smug strut. In a final gesture of defiance, mashing the lock button on the key fob with a flourish and slamming the front door behind him. The sound of the car horn signifying superiority, as if to say, ’I beat you this time.’

No one can be first all the time. If your focus is solely on getting ’the spot’, what are you missing that may be going on all around you? You had ‘the spot’ and didn’t want to give it up so you lost out on being with friends, going on that trip or having that new experience. ‘The spot’ ends up costing you. ‘The spot’ ends up controlling you. Have you actually won anything, beat anyone or gained a single thing?

Is there ‘the spot’ in your life? Something that you have allowed to elevate itself to a place of importance that overshadows other things? Take a look at what may be vying for and jockeying for first place in your life. We get what we focus on.

For where your treasure is, there will your heart be also.
(Luke 12:34)

**Date:** ______________________________

**Reflections:**

*love*

# Permeates

***Love is like a soldier who infiltrates the ranks of the opposing side, It goes behind enemy lines to rescue relationships. Love's mission is always for restoration. Love never gives up and is always worth the fight.***

## Marriage Maintenance

A marriage is like a beautiful tree. You must continue to water it for it to thrive. Care and attention keep its roots growing deeper, providing strength and security. The most important human relationship you will ever have is with your spouse. With which of these dedicated workers do you identify?

Grumpy - using your family as an audience for negative venting?

Dopey - self-medicating to handle job stress?

Doc - taking care of everyone but yourself?

Happy - faking a positive appearance at home?

Bashful - isolating and keeping all your feelings inside?

Sneezy - so run down that you are not taking care of your health?

Sleepy - either exhausted or using sleep as an escape?

Here are a few suggestions to keep your marriage well- watered.

Set aside time to reconnect - schedule it as you would any other important commitment. Write it on the calendar.

Sit next to each other, hold hands, lay your head on the other's shoulder. When possible, go to bed at the same time.

Keep a photo of the two of you together.

Cook a meal together.

Observe without judging.

Leave appreciative post-it notes for each other.

Enjoy a kiss before walking out the door and a welcome home hug when you return.

Find reasons to laugh together. Fight FOR your marriage not against each other.

That is why a man leaves his father and mother and is united to his wife, and they become one flesh.
(Genesis 2:24)

**Date:** ______________________________

**Reflections:**

*love*

# Quiets Hate

***Love is a mysterious and magnificent force that speaks in compassionate whispers and empathetic embraces, having the power to bring us together.***

## Love Thy Neighbor

I am a New Yorker, no matter where I live. I watched the World Trade Towers being built and I cried with the Nation as I watched them come down.

I am also a neuro psychotherapist and I deal with mental health and its impact on individuals, families and communities. We have a national mental health crisis. We have a national opioid epidemic. We have a rising homelessness population.

We live in a current climate where mutual hate unites people. We live in a current climate where hatred has become deadly. We are literally killing each other. We no longer tolerate people with differing opinions. We no longer listen to people with opposing views.

Because we are all born with a sin nature, we have a global sin problem. Because we are endowed with free will, evil exists in the world. Because we have a merciful Creator, we have a Savior. We have a hope.

How can we turn this around? Intentionally commit every day to being kind, compassionate, patient, gracious and loving. Neurologically speaking, embodying these qualities improves your mood by releasing positive neuro chemicals and activating the parasympathetic nervous system. Yes, it's this simple. We can love each other out of this mess.

Our experiences in this life are temporary. However, our experiences after this life are eternal. In other words, this ain't all there is.

Do not fear those who kill the body but are unable to kill the soul; but rather fear Him who is able to destroy both soul and body in hell. (Matthew 10:28 NASV)

**Date:** ______________________

**Reflections:**

*love*

# Radiates

***In its purest form, love emanates from the soul, takes up residence in the spirit and transcends the laws of physics. With every heartbeat, blood coursing through the veins, love's radiating energy flows from the top of the head through the tips of the toes.***

## Source or Err

Is there someone in your life around whom you actually feel like a better person? This is a wonderful thing. Far from internalizing that feeling and using it to boost your own ego, you are profoundly aware that this feeling is not something you keep for yourself. This feeling elevates and motivates you to give it out from yourself. This is how we are wired - to edify one another. It's a win win! The oven doesn't say, "I am great, I am heat, see I made that cake?" The heat, generated by the power supplied to the electrical components of the oven causes a reaction in the ingredients of the cake mix and BAM, there's cake!

Each part has a part in creating something amazing. (And cake is amazing!)

"...so in Christ we, though many, form one body, and each member belongs to all the others." Romans 12:5 NIV

We are created to have a part in each other's' lives. When we are mentally healthy our focus can come off ourselves and we can radiate and redirect that heat toward others.

Our source of heat, or motivation, is key to what we contribute to one another. If our source of heat is purely self-directed we manipulate and see others as stepping stones or obstacles in our way. We experience frustration, impatience and unmet expectations which lead to resentments. The greatest tragedy is that we devalue others in our effort to inflate ourselves.

"They exchanged the truth about God for a lie, and worshiped and served created things rather than the Creator--who is forever praised." Romans 1:15 NIV

The source of heat, which produces compassion and kindness, can change a person's life, can change your attitude and can change the world. Most ego-directed decisions are based on the false belief that we are the source of our own heat. The true source is the one who made you - who created within you the capacity, through connection to that source, to bring compassion and kindness to others.

Either source of that heat, whether internal or external, is infectious and can be spread rapidly. Which pandemic do you wish to live in? I not only desire to stay connected to my true source, but purpose to be that connector around whom others may say they feel like a better person. Now, let's have some of that cake!

Therefore encourage and comfort one another and build up one another, just as you are doing.
(1 Thessalonians 5:11 AMP)

**Date:** ______________________

**Reflections:**

# *love*

## Stimulates

***As electricity surges across an open wire, love can be felt as a shock to the system or as a steady, flowing current. Pulsating energy, motivating us to risk it all for the promise of love's intensity.***

## Rise and Shine

Imagine this scene...

It's bright and early on a weekday morning and you gently tip toe into your precious child's bedroom. Bending over the sleeping angel, you whisper softly in your child's ear, "Good morning, sweetheart! It's a new day, time to get up. Now remember, you're not as smart as the other children. Try not to embarrass yourself by saying something stupid. Don't forget all the mistakes you made yesterday. There really is something wrong with you and everything that goes wrong is your fault. Have an anxious day!" Ridiculous? Almost cruel to think of doing this to someone? Then why do you do this to yourself?

Listen to the way you talk to yourself. The scripts you play in your mind. Those messages are like hammers, pounding you further and further into self-loathing. So here is a literal wake-up call for you. Tomorrow morning, whether you believe the words or not, begin your day by speaking love, acceptance and grace to yourself. This is what I say every morning when I get up. "Good morning, Randi! I'm so glad we get to spend the day together. We are going to have a great time. No matter what happens, we have each other and I'll be right here with you. With our wacky sense of humor, we can always find something fun in whatever happens. So Sunshine, let's have an adventure today and a terrific story to talk about later!"

It may feel funny at first because it's kooky, but even that will have you smiling before your feet hit the floor. Just imagine what kind of a day you will have if you start smiling before your feet hit the floor!

May our Lord Jesus Christ himself and God our Father, who loved us and by his grace gave us eternal encouragement and good hope, (2 Thessalonians 2:16)

**Date:** ____________________

**Reflections:**

# *love* Translates

***There is an international language of love. Whether communicated through a smile, a touch, a gesture, an act or a word, love's meaning is never lost in translation.***

## Sweet Sleep

I believe that there are two essential beliefs which must exist in order to create an environment conducive for peaceful sleep - I am safe and I am loved.

God promises us that he is our foundation for being able to completely put our faith in them both. Repeat them after me, either in your mind or out loud: I am safe and I am loved - again, I am safe and I am loved - again, I am safe and I am loved.

I wonder if you can imagine yourself comfortably looking out on a lake. A beautiful scene, perhaps one you have experienced or one you are now having the pleasure of creating. You can feel the cool breeze coming off the water, smell the familiar scent that accompanies a lake. You hear the sounds you associate with water and nature. You look at the surface of the lake and watch the ripples in the water. Your eyes follow a small tight circular ripple and watch it as one ripple becomes two, then two ripples become three, then three ripples become four circles of water, then five circles of water. Fix your eyes on the lake as the fifth circular ripple folds back in to the fourth, and the fourth folds back into the third, and the third melts into just two ripples, and the second ripple becomes just one. Now watch as the water in the lake smooths out completely until it looks like glass. A smooth surface, completely calm, tranquil, and at peace. Imagine the feeling of these words. PERFECT PEACE.

May the God of hope fill you with all joy and peace as you trust in him, so that you may overflow with hope by the power of the Holy Spirit. (Romans 15:13)

Any person or persons in your life for whom you are carrying worry in your head, be reminded that God loves them even more than you ever could. What would it feel like to replace the worry that you feel with God's promise of hope? Take a moment and allow yourself to fill with the truth that God is in control - God is in control of everything.

God persuade me again that you are my God and that you are pursuing those whom I am so worried and consumed about with your love, even right now...I trust you LORD to take care of everything. I trust you LORD to take all my burdens right now - LORD, I give you all my burdens right now and welcome in the sweet sleep and rejuvenating rest that you love to give to me. I accept your gift of sleep and enjoy this time of refreshing.

Allow yourself to bathe in the promise of Psalm 127:2b; that God grants sleep to those he loves. God grants sleep - it is his to bestow on us.

Right now you are safe, right now you are deeply loved by your Creator God Almighty. Enjoy a sweet sleep.

When you lie down, you will not be afraid; when you lie down, your sleep will be sweet. (Proverbs 3:24)

I lie down and sleep; I wake again, because the Lord sustains me. (Psalm 3:5)

In peace I will lie down and sleep, for you alone, Lord, make me dwell in safety. (Psalm 4:8)

Come to me, all you who are weary and burdened, and I will give you rest. Take my yoke upon you and learn from me, for I am gentle and humble in heart, and you will find rest for your souls. (Matthew 11:28-29)

**Date:** ______________________

**Reflections:**

*love*

# Un-hesitates

*Once invited, love does not hold back. Love can be fearless, faultless, flawless. Love kicks down doors, moves mountains and cannot be contained.*

## Goldie Lacks

I just got sifted - sifted as wheat. came out the other side an omer short, and it feels pretty awful.

Can I blame satan for sifting me? Sure I can! His job description is all over the pages of the Bible. Remember he's wandering to and fro, seeking someone to devour. He got me. Yes, I'm sealed and my soul is secure, but my spirit is grieved tonight. Not because I behaved as the sinner I am, but because I fell short of the glory of God. In my mind, I believe I let Jesus down. I claim to be a Christ follower. I even display the cross on my body, but today I represented pride, ego and all the reasons why I need a Savior.

I haven't blown it this badly in a long time. So long that I guess I must have begun to believe my own hype. You know, feeling as though you've got this sin thing licked and this part of your life is all about being a role model for others. Pride goeth before what?

I joke about how I'm a resistant learner and God has to hold my head in the toilet and give me Cosmic Swirlies every once in a while to get my attention. Well, he got it today, and it really hurts. And maybe it should.

Now the difference to remember is to be humbled without feeling humiliated. He teaches me to be remorseful and to repent, not to remain in shame. We have an expression in addiction counseling and it is, "Shame is satan's signature."

We can be so thankful to have a Savior who loves us enough to stick with us and refine us in the fire, burning away the dross until we come forth as gold.

He causes his sun to rise on the evil and the good,
and sends rain on the righteous and the unrighteous.
(Matthew 5:45)

**Date:**

**Reflections:**

*love*

# Vibrates

*Reverberations of love reach far beyond what we can see, hear or imagine. Ripples on the surface of water, contagious laughter, the reflection of a mirror in a mirror, love replicates itself to become even more.*

## Not In Vain

I used to be a jazz and blues musician. Now, as a therapist, I help others find peace in the music of their lives. That's a career change that would give most people the bends. However, when you're already pretty twisted, nothing is off the table.

I've been around for a while and learned most of what I know from making mistakes. Plenty of twists and turns, backing up, running off the road and going in for repairs. Momma used to tell me, "Well, Randi, that's one way of getting there." It may have taken me longer, left a few more scars and given me this head of gray hair but, as the great Broadway star Elaine Stritch once sang, "I'm still here."*

One of the most important lessons I've learned is that anything we take away from those bruised knees and broken hearts is in vain if we don't share it with others. Experience is a great teacher. A degree from the School of Hard Knocks is worth framing.

Don't waste those pearls of wisdom, formed under uncomfortable circumstances, by hiding them like skeletons in your closet. Share how time and pressure produced a diamond in your character. Each of us has so much to offer. Tell your stories, your mistakes and your victories. You just may save someone from running off the road. Then both of you will be able to proudly declare, "I'm still here."

*"I'm Still Here" music & lyrics Stephen Sondheim

We love because he first loved us. (1 John 4:19)

**Date:**

**Reflections:**

*love*

# Worth the Wait

*Impatience tempts us to accept a close facsimile when we grow weary from waiting. But to be stalwart, to be relentless in pursuit, to resist the counterfeit and to hold out for the genuine, is to have it all.*

## Only Love*

All my eyes have seen
All my ears have heard
Never once assured me of love

Then I learned of one
Who had sent his son
As a ransom from up above

There has never been, nor will ever be
Such a sacrifice made for you and me

On a cross of wood
So misunderstood
By the world he died to free

Only love would go, only love would know
Only love would die for me

*"Only Love", music and lyrics Randi Konikoff

Wait for the Lord; be strong and take heart and wait for the Lord. (Psalm 27:14)

**Date:** ___

**Reflections:**

*love*

# a Xenial State

*A way to show love toward others is to offer hospitality. Sharing our homes and our families. Inviting others into our sanctuary. Expanding our lives to include the fellowship of others.*

## Sharing Joy

All of my children are back home tonight. All under the same roof. There is nothing under that Christmas tree that could thrill me more. Yes, it's crazy and stressful manipulating all the dogs, all the cars and that partridge in a pear tree. Yes, there are moments of someone getting their feathers ruffled, but there are also moments of hearing one of them whisper to the other, "I've missed you."

All of my children are here tonight, and then some! They come with spouses - Brian and Blake are wonderful additions to our family. New blood, fresh meat, new stories to enjoy and new ears to hear all of our old stories.

The house I worked so hard to clean is an instant mess. Suitcases, bags, blow up mattresses, dog beds. Stepping over PS5's (he couldn't leave home without it) and doggie tails knocking over Christmas trees. What captivating chaos. What magical madness. We pre-tested, we masked and yes we social distanced. We also smiled and laughed. We wore matching pajamas (yes, even the dogs), played silly games like 'Poop the Potato' and had glorious conversations. We laughed until we cried tears of joy and shared tears of remembrance for those who have gone on before us. We listened to holiday songs on Alexa, streamed movies on Netflix, had Zoom on the laptop, breakfast casserole in the oven and much love in the air. We shared the joy of the season with each other. We may not be hugging but the love is just as strong.

Love is the greatest gift to give and receive. Oh, and one size fits all.

Show hospitality to one another without grumbling.
(1 Peter 4:9)

**Date:** ______________________________

**Reflections:**

*love*

# Yahweh Traits

***Lavish love on our spouses, significant others, friends and all others. Lift them, edify them, encourage them. We do better, reach higher and achieve more when lovingly supported.***

## A Part or Apart

I was sitting in the waiting room of my veterinarian, waiting to take my puppy home after entropion surgery on both his eyes. The individual treatment rooms have glass panels and, if seated at just the right angle, you can see into the rooms. I noticed a woman in the room who was distraught and crying. There was a small brown dog laying on the steel table. The dog wasn't moving and it quickly became obvious as to what was happening in that room. It was like watching a silent movie. The scene unfolded with no need for sound. Her silent sobs and broken heart were conveyed through the glass and pierced my soul. I grieved for her as she draped the dog's blanket over his body, covering him completely and laying her head on his chest.

I felt I was invading her privacy, but the scene was too riveting. I felt compelled to reach out to her and offer my condolences when she came through the door. I wondered if she had anyone to give her a hug or hold her hand as she grieved.

Someone called my name and I was abruptly brought back to my purpose for being there. I paid my bill and listened to care instructions for my own puppy. Once reunited with my little guy, I scooped him up and held him extra tight.

As I walked by that glass panel I saw that the room was empty. I prayed for that woman all the way home. I pray for all those who sob in silence from any loss or heartache.

Life is going on all around us. Sorrow, joy, loneliness and love play out in a million lives every minute of every day. We can keep our head down, avoiding contact, or we can expand our awareness and share in the magnificent symphony of this global melody, played out on the strings of our hearts. Join the universal song, adding your individual descant of prayer and solidarity. Prayer is powerful, empathy draws us closer and showing compassion is the best part of being human.

My command is this: Love each other as I have loved you. (John 15:12)

**Date:** ____________________

**Reflections:**

*love*

# Zadicates

Okay, I made that one up.

*Love is the greatest power, the strongest force. It changes everything. Its absence or its presence is tangible. The secret to a rich life is no secret. It is LOVE.*

*So,*

# LoveSTRONG.

## Affirmations

I give myself unconditional love.
I lavish appreciation over myself.
I admire and embrace who I am.
I accept myself completely.
I thank God for my life.
I am kind to myself.
I am generous with praise for myself.
I esteem my abilities.
I treat myself with respect and honor.
I care for myself and provide for what I need.

It is emotionally safe to be me.

I write these things to you who believe in
the name of the Son of God so that you
may know that you have eternal life.
(1 John 5:13)

**Date:** ______________________________

**Reflections:**